W9-CMJ-473

R01628 04241

ORIOLE PARK BRANCH
DATE DUE

10/00

NOV 1 8 2000		
DEC 1 8 2000	DEC 1 5 2003	
FEB 1 7 2001	FEB 1 0 2004	
FEB 1 7 2001	MAR 1 0 2005	
MAR 1 7 2001		
APR 1 3 2001		
JUN 0 2 2001		
SEP 4 2001		
NOV 9 2001		
MAR 6 2002		
MAY 2 2 2002		
SEP 1 7 2002		
NOV 1 2002		
JAN 0 2 2003		
APR 0 2 2003		

DEMCO 38-296

DISCARD

Oriole Park Branch
7454 W. Balmoral Ave
Chicago, IL 60656

W O L F

W O L F

Wild Hunter of North America

Bruce Obee

Photography by Thomas Kitchin and Victoria Hurst

CHICAGO PUBLIC LIBRARY
ORIOLE PARK BRANCH
5201 N. OKETO   60656

Text copyright © 1994 Bruce Obee
Photographs copyright © 1994 Thomas Kitchin and Victoria Hurst

Published by Longmeadow Press, 201 High Ridge Road, Stamford, CT 06904. All rights reserved.
No part of this book may be reproduced or utilized in any form or by any means, electronic or mechanical,
including photocopying, recording or by any information storage and retrieval system,
without permission in writing from the Publisher.
Longmeadow and the colophon are registered trademarks.

First published in Canada by Key Porter Books Limited, 1994.

QL
737
.C22024
1997

PAGE 1: A CACOPHONY OF YOWLING SOUNDS IS PRODUCED WHEN WOLVES USE
WIDELY MODULATED MOVEMENTS OF THEIR JAWS AND TONGUES.

PAGE 2 AND 3: TWO FEMALE WOLVES TRY TO SCRUFF BITE EACH OTHER,
WHILE OTHER PACK MEMBERS MILL AROUND WAITING TO JOIN IN.

PAGE 4: THIS SIX-YEAR-OLD MALE IS IN THE PRIME OF LIFE.

PAGE 5: BONES ARE NOT ONLY TROPHIES TO BE DEFENDED SERIOUSLY OR IN FUN;
CHEWING ON THEM ALSO HELPS TO DEVELOP JAW AND CRANIAL MUSCLES.

PAGE 7, LEFT: HOWLING IS THE WOLF'S METHOD OF LONG-DISTANCE COMMUNICATION.

PAGE 7, RIGHT: THE EYE COLOR OF WOLVES RANGES FROM PALE GOLD TO DEEP SHADES OF BROWN.

Design: Annabelle Stanley
ISBN: 0-681-00600-5
Printed in Italy
Second Longmeadow Press Edition 1995
0 9 8 7 6 5 4 3 2

R01628 04241

CHICAGO PUBLIC LIBRARY
ORIOLE PARK
5201 N. OKETO
60656

DISCARD

CONTENTS

ENCOUNTERS

Tom KITCHIN WAS PHOTOGRAPHING CANADA GEESE IN A morning mist when the wolf appeared. It was a youngster, probably a yearling, coming up the mountain trail. Kitchin switched his 300 mm lens to autofocus and squatted to make himself look smaller.

As the wolf caught sight of him, it crouched and hesitated, sizing up the stranger on the path—was this an enemy, or something to eat? Suspiciously, the wolf raised its head, perked its ears, and timidly inched toward the photographer.

Kitchin avoided eye contact, watching the wolf through the camera. Down on his knees, he held still, speaking quietly as if to inform the wolf, "I'm human."

"Your body language is all important. You're telegraphing constantly to an animal whose survival depends on interpreting the movements of other animals.

"Predators move swiftly. If you let your excitement and your adrenalin overcome you, the animal that you're trying to photograph is very aware that you are moving like a predator. Quick movements and they're gone."

Cautious but curious, the wolf crept closer—twenty paces, fifteen . . . until the lens would no longer focus. "At that point he was 10 feet (3 m) away. I was shooting full-framed head shots of him."

LEFT: A YEARLING MALE IN THE FALL.

The inquisitive wolf approached within two arm's-lengths, apprehensive but apparently unafraid, wondering how to get past the obstacle on the trail. Neither animal moved: it was a standoff.

"I was on my knees and thought, 'What the hell.' I dropped down onto my hands, so I was at the wolf's level, and started to howl. He stood next to me and began to howl with me. There the two of us are at sunrise, howling like two fools."

One-on-one meetings like this are rare. Only in parks where hunting is prohibited, and in the remotest wildlands, where animals haven't learned to distrust humans, are people likely to enjoy close encounters with wolves. Except on open tundra, a common wolf sighting is a fleeting glimpse of a rear end vanishing into the bush.

Kitchin's wolf, in Jasper National Park, Alberta, eventually sauntered past him and continued along the trail. Neither wolf nor photographer exhibited any fear. Kitchin has photographed many wild wolves, but, ironically, the only time he has felt afraid was when shooting captive wolves.

He and his wife, Vicki Hurst, were in a wooded enclosure at the Canadian Centre for Wolf Research in Nova Scotia. They'd been deposited there by biologists who told them to sit patiently on the ground; the wolves would emerge from the woods.

"We were feeling faintly ridiculous," Kitchin recalls. "You don't know what's coming." Eventually three pairs of eyes peered inquisitively from behind the trees.

"We were told not to make a lot of eye contact. So we're sort of staring at our hiking boots and these wolves are starting to circle us—circling as if we're a prey species." Both seasoned wildlife photographers, Hurst and Kitchin had watched wild wolves approaching carcasses, slinking up slowly, ready to retreat at the slightest motion. These captive wolves showed similar trepidation.

"Finally a wolf came up to Vicki and started to rub his head all over her hiking boots, back and forth. Then this other wolf came up to her and rubbed all over the back of her parka. Vicki's laughing and giggling, really enjoying herself, and the third wolf came up and started rubbing on her knees." Kitchin soon got the same treatment, and the uncertainty of their initial introduction faded.

"If I've ever had a feeling of fear around wolves, there was a smidgen when we were sitting there waiting for them, not knowing what their next step was going to be."

Inviting such intimate contact with wolves would have been considered tantamount to suicide only a few decades ago. These predators have been feared by humans since ancient times. By the mid-1900s, the centuries-old war on the wolf had almost been won: they'd been eliminated or reduced to remnant populations across most of North America. Now, only three decades since the last bounties were paid, a movement to restore the wolf to its traditional range is gathering momentum.

The gray or timber wolf (*Canis lupus*) was once the most widely distributed land mammal in the northern hemisphere. In North America it ranged from Mexico to the Arctic, inhabiting the forests, plains, and tundra from coast to coast. Today the gray wolf numbers fewer than two thousand in the contiguous United States. A Mexican subspecies, *Canis lupus baileyi*, has nearly vanished from the wild. Captive populations may be its only hope. The future of the red wolf (*Canis rufus*), a native of the southeastern states, is also dependent on captive breeding. Except in Minnesota, all wolves in the lower forty-eight states are endangered.

In Canada and Alaska there is more reason for optimism. In all, there may be seventy thousand gray wolves north of the forty-ninth parallel. Although their comeback is impressive, they have not yet repopulated much of their historic range in the Maritimes, on the island of Newfoundland, or in southern regions of the central and eastern provinces.

The vast tracts of wilderness that once stretched across the continent are no longer continuous. Cities, farms and industries have irreversibly altered the habitat for wolves and their prey. The landscape now is disjunct; the natural travel corridors are broken by highways, buildings, pipelines, and other man-made amenities.

These things can't be changed, so expectations of a full recovery for the North American wolf are unrealistic. But human perspectives can change: the myths and misconceptions about the ways of the wolf are gradually being dispelled. As the importance of predators in natural ecosystems becomes more widely recognized, the wolf will regain its stature in the North American wilderness.

OPPOSITE PAGE: WOLVES ARE ELUSIVE BY NATURE, WHICH MAKES THEM EXTREMELY DIFFICULT TO OBSERVE IN THE WILD. THIS WOLF WAS PHOTOGRAPHED WITH A 300 MM TELEPHOTO LENS IN ALASKA'S DENALI NATIONAL PARK, CONSIDERED BY MANY WILDLIFE PHOTOGRAPHERS TO BE THE BEST PLACE IN NORTH AMERICA TO SEE WILD WOLVES.

ABOVE: Footprints are one of the few signs that wolves are in an area.
Naturalists can determine the number, direction, speed,
and some of the behavior of wolves travelling together from tracks.

❧

OPPOSITE PAGE: A glimpse through the trees of an adult male in
the Rocky Mountains. Surrounded by forest, he is attuned
to the sounds, sights, and smells that make up his world.

ABOVE: WOLVES HAVE EXCELLENT HEARING; THEY CAN DETECT SOUNDS FROM
MILES AWAY EVEN IN FORESTED AREAS. THEIR ABILITY TO ORIENT THEIR EARS
INDEPENDENTLY HELPS TO LOCALIZE SOUNDS.

❧

RIGHT: WHY WOLVES RUB THEMSELVES IN STRONG ODORS IS STILL A MYSTERY TO
RESEARCHERS WHO HAVE STUDIED THE PHENOMENON. TO THE DISMAY OF MANY DOG OWNERS,
THE BEHAVIOR IS PERSISTENT DESPITE CENTURIES OF DOMESTICATION.

BECAUSE WOLVES RELY PRIMARILY ON MOVEMENT DETECTION FOR
MUCH OF THEIR VISUAL ACUITY, IT IS SOMETIMES DIFFICULT FOR THEM TO DISCERN
SOMETHING THAT IS STANDING STILL (LIKE THE PHOTOGRAPHER).
WHEN WOLVES BOB THEIR HEADS UP AND DOWN, THEY MAY BE TRYING TO
CREATE AN "ARTIFICIAL MOVEMENT" TO GIVE THEM A BETTER
SENSE OF WHAT THEY ARE SEEING.

RIGHT: THE BLACK FACE OF THIS YOUNG MALE ACCENTUATES HIS GOLDEN EYES.

BELOW: WOLVES OFTEN COOL OFF IN WATER OR INCORPORATE IT INTO THEIR PLAY.
THEY SEEM TO DELIGHT IN ROMPING THROUGH SHALLOWS.

DRAWN BY CURIOSITY, THIS FEMALE WOLF IS READY TO FLEE AT
ANY SUDDEN MOVEMENT FROM THE PHOTOGRAPHER.

THE EYES OF THIS MALE FOLLOW EVERY MOVE THE PHOTOGRAPHER MAKES.

ALTHOUGH VISION MAY NOT BE THE MOST IMPORTANT OF THE WOLF'S SENSES,

WOLVES RELY ON IT IN CLOSE ENCOUNTERS.

THE SEASON OF BIRTH

IN THE COOL OF A MID-SPRING DAWN, A WOLF PUP EMERGES from a hole in a hillside and squints at the rising sun. It shudders as a chill morning breeze ruffles its downlike fur. Tempted by curiosity, it begins to totter down the hill, but its maiden outing is cut short by its mother. The pup is carted by the head back to the safety of the burrow.

Nourished only by their mother's milk, this infant wolf and its siblings have huddled in the darkness of their den for nearly three weeks, oblivious to the daylight beyond. From birth they have felt the moist, warm caress of their mother's tongue cleansing their fragile forms. Blind and deaf, they stumbled over one another to find the teats that stem their hunger.

A blissful scene—a mother suckling her offspring in the first days of life.

LEFT: PUPS CAN VARY IN HEIGHT AND WEIGHT EVEN WITHIN THE SAME LITTER.
PUPS THAT WERE SMALL AS INFANTS MAY CATCH UP TO, AND EVEN SURPASS,
THEIR SIBLINGS IN SIZE BEFORE THEY REACH MATURITY.

23

But there is a harshness behind the scene: some of this litter have already died. Like the afterbirth, the dead pups were eaten by the mother.

At this early age these pups are oblivious to the hierarchical rules of wolf society. But as they grow toward sexual maturity, there will be clearer divisions between weak and strong. Eventually one could rise to become the alpha male or female—a breeder—another may be relegated to life as an underdog.

The annual addition of pups to a wolf pack is the result of an elaborate courtship between the alpha pair. These are the leaders, and though there is some debate about whether the alpha male or female rules supreme, these two wolves most often dominate the pack's activities, from howling to hunting and feeding. In cases where two wandering wolves unite to form a new pack, they become the leaders by default.

Although wild females may give birth at the age of two or three, many bear their first litter when four or five years old. Mating age may be determined not only by sexual maturity, but also by the ability of a breeder to secure a partner and maintain a territory.

Across North America, breeding seasons vary with latitudes: mating begins between late February and mid-March in the northern United States and southern Canada; in Alaska, the Yukon, Northwest Territories, and other colder climes, it starts in late March or early April.

During a proestrus stage, lasting from one to seven weeks before she comes into estrus, the female enters a state peculiar to coyotes, dogs, and wolves in which she bleeds from the vagina, imparting her condition to her mate. Their bond is then stengthened by double scent-marking: the alpha male urinates over blood and urine stains left by his partner on trees, rocks, snowbanks, and other landmarks within the territory. The marking rate increases, with new pairs especially zealous, as mating approaches.

Throughout the breeding period the affection between the alpha pair becomes more noticeable. They groom each other, touch frequently, travel side by side over long distances. The loyalty born of these mating rituals is not unique, but is certainly uncommon in the mammalian world. One mournful Mexican wolf returned each night for more than two weeks to a site where its mate had been trapped. The distraught wolf's grief ended on the sixteenth night when it too was caught.

Researchers once believed monogamy was the adhesive that so strongly bonded the alpha pair. But observations of both wild and captive wolves suggest infidelity is not unheard-of among breeders. Alphas have been known to part company and seek other mates, sometimes subordinates from within the pack.

It is more common, however, for the dominant pair to thwart the amorous pursuits of subordinates. The alpha male asserts his authority over libidinous underlings with snarls, growls and other threats. Would-be mothers vying for the affections of the alpha male are aggressively dissuaded by the alpha female.

The alphas control the birthrate according to environmental circumstances. If food is scarce or the pack is already large, they may be more earnest in discouraging subordinate breeding. If mortality is high or prey is abundant, there is less reason to inhibit mating among lower-ranking wolves.

A female not in full heat resists the advances of her suitor by sitting on her tail or folding it between her legs. When the time for intercourse arrives, the pair may move away from the main pack, but sometimes other wolves linger about to witness the event. When the male mounts its mate from behind, the two are joined and are unable to separate for up to thirty minutes. This copulatory tie, an idiosyncrasy of some canines, is caused by the female's vaginal sphincter muscles contracting around the male's swollen penis. The male then swings his body around by placing his front legs to one side of his partner and lifting a hind leg over her back. They remain fused, tail to tail, until the female is inseminated.

While some researchers say finding a den site is the pregnant wolf's responsibility, others believe both the father and mother select and dig the den. The ideal locale is near fresh water, preferably with a wooded area adjacent to open land where prey can be easily spotted. Dens are often located on high ground where they are less likely to be flooded and there are good views of surrounding terrain.

Some wolves simply move into an unused cave. Others enlarge the deserted burrow of another animal. Many are excavated from scratch and used year after year, sometimes for decades. A mound of earth accumulates at the den entrance as the parent-to-be energetically digs with front feet, shooting dirt and debris out between its legs.

A wolf-sized tunnel, from 6 to 14 feet (2-4 m) long, leads to an enlarged whelping chamber. The deeper the den, the harder it is for unwelcome visitors to detect the activity inside. Other passageways, some with separate entrances, may branch off the tunnel. A web of well-worn trails radiates from the main entrance, which is usually oval-shaped and about 2 feet (0.6 m) in diameter. This entrance is generally adorned by the largest pile of dirt.

The pupping chamber lies uphill from the entrance to avoid flooding. It is not lined with bedding material and some scientists surmise that wolves intentionally leave the interior barren to dissuade fleas from laying their eggs inside. Droppings left by the pups are eaten by the mother.

The pregnant wolf completes her excavation three or four weeks before the births. After sixty-three days' gestation, litters of five, six, seven pups or more are born in spring. Their arrival is celebrated by a great deal of noise and commotion among pack members outside the den. It is during the season of birth that the wolf pack's entity as a family is most evident. All share in the upbringing of the youngsters—feeding, babysitting, protecting them from intruders. Fortunately, the pups are born at a time when hunting is comparatively simple: by the end of winter, prey species are at their weakest, making them easy targets for wolves with pups to feed. And like the wolves, prey with new offspring are unable to move long distances, keeping them within reasonable reach of well-selected den sites.

When prey is abundant, a subordinate female occasionally bears a litter that is accepted by the pack. These pups may merge with those of the alpha female to be fed by both mothers. In 1988 at Alaska's Denali National Park a subordinate wolf raised a litter about a mile (1.6 km) from the main den. After a month she carried them, one by one, to the pack's main burrow where they were raised with the other pups. Sometimes pups are fed by pseudopregnant females. Most sexually mature, non-breeding bitches enter a hormonal state similar to pregnancy in which they produce milk. They may lactate in response to a pup suckling.

While nursing mothers are tied to home, other pack members bring them fresh or regurgitated food. Caring for a mother and offspring is an example of the unflinching devotion shown by the pack throughout the birthing season. In one instance at Denali National Park a pregnant wolf wandered too far from the den and was compelled to bear her young on the tundra. Unable to move the pups for a full day, she was fed snowshoe hares by some family members, while others stood guard over the newborns. Yet even with help from the entire pack, large litters of twelve or fourteen rarely survive: at least half die of malnutrition, diseases, and other causes.

For animals that encroach upon an occupied den, wolves are formidable foes. In 1990 Alaskan wolves hunted down and killed three grizzly bears that had come uncomfortably close to a den. Wolves rarely challenge a grizzly at a kill site, but the incident proves that they are fearless in defense of their families.

With a stubby muzzle and legs, brown or slate-black coat, and folded ears, a newborn wolf looks somewhat like a cross between a fur seal and a black bear cub. About the size of a city squirrel, it measures 10 to 13 inches (25–33 cm) from head to tail and weighs less than a pound (0.45 kg).

For the first ten or twelve days, the sightless pups blunder about the den, preoccupied with latching onto one of their mother's eight teats. Before the end of the second week they begin to view their underground lair through inquisitive blue eyes. A week later their world is widened by another sense— hearing. Whether wolves are born with a keen sense of smell is a debatable point among researchers: some believe it develops over time; others say pups use olfactory senses from birth to locate a mother's teats and strengthen the parental bond.

Nova Scotia researchers eavesdropped on a captive wolf den with remotely operated equipment. It was discovered that pups begin cooing like human babies moments after birth, emitting repetitive, harmonic vocalizations. Barks produced on their first day were difficult to distinguish from those of adults when examined visually on voice prints. Distinct "woofs" and high-pitched calls known as "social squeaks" were heard as the pups' eyes and ears became functional and their motor skills improved. Around the fourth week, probably as their voice boxes developed, howls were heard. It was concluded that all vocalizations of adult wolves are made by pups before they leave the den. Interestingly, many of these noises were made by pups who had neither heard nor seen adult wolves making the same sounds.

Around the third week the pups' milk teeth break through; the young wolves begin to eat food regurgitated by pack members. The mother enjoys brief hunting excursions, leaving her offspring in the care of another family member. Timid and shaky in the knees, the pups begin to explore outside the den, venturing short distances from the entrance, scurrying back at any perceived danger. They wrestle with their denmates, developing muscles and motor skills.

The pups' boldness grows with their bodies; at four or five weeks they wander farther from the den. Food-bearing adults are welcomed excitedly as the pups beg to be fed, licking the muzzles and nipping the cheeks of adults. Some researchers view food-begging as an early act of submission, which later plays an important role in pack life.

By the sixth week their roly-polyness has all but vanished. Legs and bodies are longer; the bluntness is stretched from their muzzles. Adult hair is growing over their bodies. The eyes of many begin to turn yellow, revealing a hint of the intent glare that dominant wolves often use to stare down subordinates. Howling becomes frequent, and they regularly travel up to a mile (1.6 km) with the pack. They are starting to look and act like wolves.

At the age of two months, after they're weaned, healthy pups may weigh 15 or 20 pounds (7 or 9 kg). With well-developed teeth, they chew voraciously on bones and sticks, and peel bark from trees. They frantically shake things in their teeth, chase other animals and practise pouncing on make-believe mice.

There's an urgency to the growth of wolf pups: like their prey, the search for food keeps wolves constantly on the move. By early summer the pups must be strong enough to travel to rendezvous sites, places near sources of food and water where the hunters gather to share their quarry with the pups.

It is at these sites that young wolves bone up on their hunting skills by catching small prey. Though playful in appearance, this is serious business: at three or four months, pups have learned to associate killing with eating. They are old enough to join hunting parties as observers, but not until the age of six months, when they actually look like adult wolves, are they able to help in the kill. By early autumn all wolves in the pack must travel great distances to keep their bellies filled.

As it grows toward sexual maturity at twenty-two months, a juvenile wolf develops a leeriness of strangers. Strong emotional ties to its own pack are established: outsiders are not to be trusted. Once a young wolf inherits this wariness, it acquires the true soul of a wolf.

OPPOSITE PAGE: THE MT. MCKINLEY AREA IN ALASKA IS WELL KNOWN FOR ITS WOLVES. OVER FIFTY YEARS AGO, THE PIONEERING WOLF BIOLOGIST ADOLPH MURIE CONDUCTED THE FIRST SCIENTIFIC STUDY OF A PACK'S SOCIAL LIFE AT A DEN SITE NEAR HERE.

❧

INSET: PUPS SPEND THE FIRST FEW WEEKS OF LIFE INSIDE THE PROTECTION OF THE DEN BUT VENTURE OUTSIDE FOR SHORT FORAYS AS SOON AS THEY ARE STRONG ENOUGH TO MAKE THEIR WAY TO THE TUNNEL ENTRANCE. THE EMERGENCE OF THE PUPS IS A BIG EVENT FOR THE REST OF THE PACK, WHICH LAVISHES THEM WITH ATTENTION.

RIGHT: THIS THREE-WEEK-OLD MALE PUP LIES ON TOP
OF ITS NATAL DEN AND SURVEYS ITS NEW WORLD.
AS IT GROWS OLDER, IT WILL MAKE MORE AND MORE
EXTENDED EXCURSIONS AWAY FROM THE DEN,
USUALLY IN THE COMPANY OF OTHER PUPS
OR OLDER PACK MEMBERS.

OPPOSITE PAGE: AS THE PUPS GET OLDER, THE MOTHER IS MORE LIKELY TO
NURSE THEM OUTSIDE THE DEN THAN INSIDE. SHE CALLS THEM OUT WITH A SQUEAKING
VOCALIZATION AT THE DEN ENTRANCE. IF MORE THAN ONE LITTER IS BORN TO A PACK,
THE MOTHERS USUALLY POOL THE PUPS AND TAKE TURNS NURSING THE COMBINED LITTER.

ABOVE: THIS PUP STILL HAS THE BLUE EYES OF INFANCY.
PUPS ARE BORN WITH THEIR EYES TIGHTLY SHUT AND THEIR EARS FLATTENED
AGAINST THEIR HEADS. THEIR EYES ARE OPEN BY TWO WEEKS OF AGE,
AND THEY CAN HEAR AT ABOUT THREE WEEKS.

ৰ

OPPOSITE PAGE: ADULTS CARRY PUPS BY HOLDING THEM FIRMLY BY
THEIR HEADS, NECKS, OR BACKS. THIS PUP IS GETTING TOO BIG TO BE PICKED UP,
BUT THE MOTHER USES THE SAME GRIP TO PULL IT ALONG THE GROUND.

THE NATURAL FEATURES OF THEIR SURROUNDINGS ARE INCORPORATED INTO WOLF PLAY.

THIS TEN-WEEK-OLD PUP WAITS TO AMBUSH ANOTHER FROM BEHIND A TREE.

All adult wolves are hormonally primed to care for pups in the spring.

Aunts and uncles as well as yearling brothers and sisters regurgitate or

carry food to the den, and groom, defend, and play with the pups.

LEFT: PUPS DEPEND ON THEIR OLDER FAMILY MEMBERS TO
BRING FOOD TO THE DEN AND RENDEZVOUS SITE.
IT WILL BE MONTHS BEFORE THESE YOUNG WOLVES
CAN HUNT SUCCESSFULLY ON THEIR OWN.

❧

BELOW: THREE PUPS TRY TO GAIN POSSESSION OF A
SCRAP OF MEAT, PULLING UNTIL ONE GIVES WAY OR
IT COMES APART AND THEY EACH GET A PIECE.
PUPS ALSO PLAY GAMES OF TUG OF WAR WITH PIECES
OF DEER SKIN, STICKS, BONES, AND OTHER OBJECTS.

Young wolves are seldom seriously aggressive toward one another

until they reach sexual maturity in their second winter.

The two pups on the left show signs of mild aggression in competition

over a piece of food — the raised tail and intent gaze of the standing pup,

and the slightly narrowed eyes and wrinkled muzzle of the prone one.

39

IN ANTICIPATION OF BEING FED, AN ENTHUSIASTIC YOUNGSTER
TRIPS AN ADULT RETURNING TO REGURGITATE FOOD AT THE RENDEZVOUS SITE.

RIGHT: WOLVES DO NOT LIKE TO EAT THE LONG HAIR OF WHITE-TAILED DEER; THEY PLUCK IT OFF THE CARCASS OR PULL OFF PIECES OF HIDE. LATER THE PIECES OF HIDE MAKE GOOD TOYS FOR PUPS.

BELOW: THE LATE SPRING IS A BLISSFUL TIME FOR A YOUNG PUP LUCKY ENOUGH TO BE BORN WHEN THERE IS SUFFICIENT FOOD FOR ALL THE PACK AND NO IMMEDIATE DANGERS.

ABOVE: The baby face of this two-month-old female is beginning to lengthen into a more grownup look. Although she can now move with much better coordination than she could as an infant, she will retain the clumsiness characteristic of pups for some time.

❧

OPPOSITE PAGE: The availability of water to drink is an important consideration in the location of dens and rendezvous sites. Wolves will sometimes move pups to be closer to a water source.

ABOVE: AN ADOLESCENT MALE LOOKS CURIOUSLY AT THE PHOTOGRAPHER.
THE HAIR SURROUNDING THE LIPS OF WOLF PUPS AND SUBADULTS IS DARK
AND MAKES THEM LOOK LIKE THEY ARE GRINNING.

LEFT: TWO FEMALE YEARLINGS HAVE JUST PLAYED A BIT TOO
ROUGH WITH AN EIGHT-MONTH-OLD PUP. HE LOOKS OVER HIS SHOULDER AS IF TO SAY,
IS THIS STILL PLAY? YEARLINGS MUST LEARN TO TEMPER THEIR PLAY WITH
YOUNGER SIBLINGS, ESPECIALLY WHEN THE PUPS ARE SMALL.

45

LIFE IN
THE PACK

UNDER THE CRISP BLUE LIGHT OF A WINTER MOON THE hush over a woodland lake is suddenly displaced by the singular howl of a wolf. Pure and sonorous, almost tangible, it rings like a bugle summoning dogs to a hunt.

Then all is still. But the reprieve is momentary, for the unsettling call of another lone wolf, as distinctive as the laughter of a loon, echoes an answer from the opposite shore.

The first wolf, a virile young male, anxiously trots through the trees toward the lakehead. It stops, lifts its muzzle to the moon and repeats its vibrant cry. Before the song subsides the second voice joins the chorus. Both wolves quicken the pace and close the gap between them.

Neither is surprised by this encounter. In their wanderings their paths have crossed in the snow. They have grown familiar with the scented calling cards placed along the trail.

LEFT: THESE TWO ADULTS, CAUGHT IN MID-GALLOP, ARE OUT FOR A PLAYFUL RUN ON A FALL DAY.

Instinctively, they approach with apprehension. Both in their third year, they have learned to mistrust all but their own kin. But these wolves, for whatever reason, have forsaken their families to seek their own partners and places. Their inherent timidity is quelled by a subtle jubilation. Tails wagging, nostrils flared, lips pulled back in a grin, they whine and sniff, touch noses and lick each other's face. The search is over; a new pack is formed.

Had these wolves been of the same sex they might have joined forces to hunt, but probably would have gone separate ways. As a new pair, however, their quest now is to find a territory in which to raise their young. Wary of trespassing, they will be constantly on the lookout as they roam—watching, listening, sniffing urine-soaked scent marks that conspicuously display the boundaries of entrenched packs. Eventually they will find a home of their own.

A new pair, the most basic pack, is the foundation on which the intricate society of wolves is built. Unlike deer, moose, or most other creatures, wolves are not abandoned to the wilderness within their first year. Instead, they remain in close-knit families, enjoying the company of their parents and siblings for generations. Some wolves never leave their original packs.

In North America the wolf is the primary predator of big animals. Its penchant for moose, elk, deer, caribou, musk-oxen and other prey larger than itself creates a need for hunting efficiency and safety in numbers. Though a hardy hundred-pound (45 kg) wolf can single-handedly fell a moose ten times its size, it invariably fares better as a member of a team. Even with the help of packmates, many a wolf suffers a fractured skull or spine with one well-aimed kick from a heavy hoof.

Propagation is the simplest way for a two-member pack to boost its wolf-power. With litters averaging six pups, a pack of two could become fourteen by the second breeding season. But mortality among wild animals is high, often 50 percent or more. It's likely that this pack would number only six or eight after the wilderness takes its toll.

Surviving pups don't mature until twenty-two months, so when the second breeding season arrives their sexual inadequacy makes for peace within the pack. By the next season, however, the young of the first year are capable, and frequently keen, to produce their own offspring. Sexual conflicts caused by attempts to mate with parents or siblings can be severe enough to split the pack: young wolves eager to produce their own offspring may set off in search of a mate. Those that fail may surreptitiously tail the old pack, living on scraps abandoned for ravens and other scavengers. If willing to abide the affronts of the ruling pair, a defector may be permitted to rejoin its original pack.

Despite internal strife, a pack is generally a gregarious group whose unity stems from the wolf's ability to form emotional ties. Anyone who has witnessed the care and affection bestowed upon newborn pups by all pack members, or watched wolves of all ages romping around an open field, appreciates the affability within this animal's family.

As in all families though, there is conflict. Through the so-called pecking order, the status of individuals within a pack is defined. Age is the principal determinant, putting the parents—the alpha pair—at the top. Though the alphas are the dominant wolves, whether they are the leaders in virtually every way is a debatable point among wolf biologists. Field observations, however, show that they are often first to howl before a hunt, first to attack prey, first to eat from a fresh kill, first to ward off threats against the pack. Usually larger and stronger than the others, they run at the head of the line, breaking trail through winter snow for the others who follow in single file. When exercising their dominance, the alpha female disciplines the females while her partner intimidates the males.

When an alpha wolf becomes too old to breed, it may remain with the pack but could be replaced by the next in line—the beta. Sometimes the transition occurs without incident: other times there's bloodshed. If an alpha wolf dies, its partner may secure a new mate from outside the pack, obliging subordinates to accept a newcomer.

Though the alphas are at the top, the social order in a wolf pack is not always clear. Generally, the alphas dominate the betas and younger wolves. Middle-ranking wolves may be hard to define, but wolves who hold the unenviable position of an omega, a Greek word meaning "last," are easy to pinpoint. This scapegoat bears the brunt of the whole family's aggression: it is common for an omega to become an outcast, to quietly slip away from the interminable abuse.

Throughout life, wolves repeatedly demonstrate their deference to those of higher rank by acts of submission. Body movements, facial expressions, and sounds convey their respect. When a dominant wolf presents an overblown image by approaching with raised hackles, ears, and tail, a subordinate's response is to hold still and lower its tail, ears, and body. Serious fights or injuries are rare in these showdowns.

In many clashes the dominant animal's most effective weapon is not physical but psychological—a penetrating stare. Such an unsettling expression transmits a menacing unpredictability—there's no telling what this wolf might do. This classic pose adorns the cover of the book *Of Wolves and Men*, in which author Barry Lopez says the wolf "takes your stare and turns it back on you." The Bella Coola of Canada's west coast believed the wolf's humanlike stare was the result of a failed attempt to turn all animals into people. While all the creatures remained unchanged, the eyes of the wolf became human.

Effective as it may be, a stony stare isn't always enough to maintain order in an exceptionally large pack. The ability, or inability, of the alpha pair to assert its dominance probably has some bearing on pack size. Other factors might be the degree of hierarchical competition, or the number of wolves that could reasonably form social attachments to others.

Food is another factor. In Alaska, where prey is plentiful, packs of twenty or more are common. The largest pack on record numbered thirty-six Alaskan wolves. Such superpacks, however, are seldom seen all hunting together or sharing one kill. While half a dozen wolves are more efficient than one or two in downing large prey, more than five or six hunters provide little extra help. Big packs are apt to split into smaller groups for a few hours, or days, and hunt separate parts of a common territory.

These temporary hunting squads may be comprised of members holding similar social status. With higher-ranking wolves taking first crack at the carcass, little is left sometimes for hungry subordinates. They either catch their own food or starve.

Such stiff competition within one pack can cause the permanent dispersal of some members, particularly in autumn and early winter, when packs are largest after a breeding season. New packs may seek unoccupied hunting grounds or usurp part of the original pack's territory. As boundaries are realigned, related wolves become rivals.

It's probable that lone wolves are also products of internal strife. Such pariahs shadow their old packs, falling several days and miles behind, risking harassment from stronger animals as they scrounge for leftovers. Other lone wolves might be old alphas who have lost their mates and are not likely to breed again. Loners tend to linger on the edges of other wolves' territories, covering ten or twenty times as much ground as packs. Careful to avoid skirmishes with established packs, they may wander for months before finding somewhere to settle.

In his book *The Wolf*, biologist David Mech suggests that social pressures are more important than food in controlling pack size. A wolf's stomach can hold 15 or 19 pounds (7 or 9 kg) of meat, says Mech, so a 150-pound (68 kg) deer could feed approximately ten wolves. An 800-pound (363 kg) moose could feed forty or fifty wolves, yet packs that eat deer are usually of comparable size to those that eat moose. It also seems that the size of prey has little relevance to the size of pack.

The migratory habits and amount of prey, however, does govern the size of a territory. Where deer are plentiful, one pack may find enough food in a 30-square-mile (78 km²) area. If nomadic herds of caribou are the mainstay, a single wolf pack might patrol a thousand square miles (2600 km²). In Alaska, one pack reportedly travelled 5,000 square miles (13 000 km²) over six weeks.

Few animals can match the wolf mile for mile in their daily travels. Averaging 5 to 9 miles (8–14 km) an hour, a wolf may roam 20 miles (32 km) or more to bring back food for pups in a den. A pack of seven Arctic wolves, followed in an all-terrain vehicle, wandered 30 miles (48 km) from a den to take a musk-ox. A pack of fifteen wolves tracked by air in Michigan's Isle Royale National Park moved more than 30 miles (48 km) a day while hunting moose.

With such large hunting grounds, some wolves visit parts of their territories only once or twice a year. Unlike borders on a map, the boundaries of wolf territories are neither permanent nor clearly defined. Territories are separated by buffer zones, where no pack claims ownership.

Despite ambiguous borders, wolf territories are continuously marked by their occupants. During winter, when wolves are constantly on the move, they urinate and defecate frequently. Borders are marked about twice as heavily as the centers of territories. Females seem to scent-mark less often than males, but both alpha wolves raise their legs to lift the marks above the ground. Some wolves kick dirt over scent posts to accentuate the marking. Wolves, which bury food for later use, also mark empty food caches, a signal to others that there's nothing left to plunder.

With its acute sense of smell, a wolf can sniff out a two-week-old scent mark. The olfactory area in a wolf's skull is fourteen times as large as a human's, giving it about a hundred times more scent power. In favorable winds a wolf can detect an animal 300 yards (274 m) away.

While scent-marking tells where a wolf has been, howling broadcasts where it is. Chorus howls, like bird songs, warn potential intruders against trespassing. On clear days in open terrain the howl of a wolf can be heard 6 miles (10 km) away. Some researchers believe wolves modulate their voices to exaggerate the size of a pack.

Whether one pack replies to the calls of another depends on circumstances. Wolves trying to avoid confrontation are likely to answer the howls of a neighboring pack. Wolves in need of food from an adjoining territory may not respond to their neighbors' calls, saving the option of launching a silent invasion.

In Minnesota's Superior National Forest, wolves that did not reply to another pack's howls were seen marching along a trail directly toward the territory's occupants. In at least two of these encounters, resident wolves were attacked and killed. In another, the resident pack was disbanded and its territory was commandeered by the assailants.

Perhaps observations of these intraspecific conflicts led to early misconceptions about the wolf's supposedly vicious nature. The Rev. J. G. Wood, a well-known nineteenth-century British naturalist, described the wolf this way:

> It is by no means nice in its palate, and will eat almost any living animal—from human beings down to frogs, lizards, and insects. Moreover, it is a sad cannibal, and is thought by several travellers who have noted its habits to be especially partial to the flesh of its own kind. A weak, sickly, or wounded wolf is sure to fall under the cruel teeth of its companions; who are said to be so fearfully ravenous that if one of their companions should chance to besmear himself with the blood of the prey which has just been hunted down, he is instantly attacked and devoured by the remainder of the pack.

Modern science has dispelled many old misinterpretations of the wolf's habits, yet some traits remain unexplained. In *Trail of the Wolf*, biologist R. D. Lawrence describes three of his own observations of territorial feuds:

> In each case, the two alpha males, watched expectantly by their companions, approached each other, tails erect and hackles raised.

They walked stiff-legged, but slowly, towards each other, and when they were almost nose to nose, both began to play, gamboling around the small clearing where the meeting had taken place. They jumped over each other, knocking one another to the ground, and then raced around in circles.

Another time, however, Lawrence watched a resident pack repel invaders, badly injuring a young male. Whether the outcomes of these meetings are determined by food supply, genetics, or other factors is unknown.

It could be that the wolf is simply not a fighter at heart, defending its turf and family against selected adversaries only when left with no choice. Adolph Murie, who studied Alaskan wolves in the 1940s, crawled into a den and kidnapped a pup. The alpha pair barked and howled, but did not attack. Two men on Ellesmere Island, in the Canadian Arctic, captured two pups and were followed to their camp by a big female. In spite of attempts to drive her off, she remained outside the tent all night, but did not attack.

Maybe wolves are aggressive to other wolves and predators, but avoid confrontation with humans. In extremely remote places, like Ellesmere Island, limited contact with people has given wolves little reason to fear them. In the more populated south, centuries of persecution have made wild wolves justifiably wary of humans.

David Mech, probably the world's foremost authority on wolves, describes his favorite species as "one of the wildest and shyest of all the animals in the northern wilderness." Many seasoned outback wanderers share a lifetime in close proximity to wolves and never see one. On Isle Royale, which has one of North

America's highest wolf densities, Mech hiked 1,400 miles (2253 km) over four summers and saw wolves only three times. "In all cases, the animals ran off so quickly and silently that I was left wondering if I had really seen them."

Loathed or loved, the wolf's elusiveness and social nature have captivated people since ancient times. Perhaps there is some kind of subliminal mammalian bond between humans and wolves: *Homo sapiens* and *Canis lupus* are, after all, among the few species on Earth to have families.

OPPOSITE PAGE: BOREAL FORESTS, WITH THEIR ABUNDANCE OF PLANT AND ANIMAL LIFE,
ARE PRIME HABITAT FOR WOLVES. ONLY LARGE TRACTS OF WILDERNESS
CAN PROVIDE WOLVES AND OTHER LARGE PREDATORS WITH
A WIDE ENOUGH PREY BASE TO SUSTAIN THEM.

INSET: A PACK OF WOLVES IS AN EXTENDED FAMILY UNIT CONSISTING OF PARENTS,
OFFSPRING OF VARIOUS AGES, AND SOMETIMES AUNTS AND UNCLES.
THEIR DEEP, LONG-LASTING SOCIAL BONDS AND COOPERATIVE
LIFESTYLE PARALLEL THAT OF HUMANS.

LEFT: To the amazement of the photographer, this wild yearling male approached him within 10 feet (3 m). Subadult wolves leave their packs to explore their surroundings and develop their hunting skills. This is a time of high mortality for many young wolves because they have not yet learned to fear humans and new experiences.

৵

OPPOSITE PAGE: Being part of a pack is of the utmost importance to wolves; nonetheless, each member is very much an individual in personality and appearance. At first glance, these gray wolves look alike, but they are easily distinguished by their different faces and the markings on their backs, shoulders, and tails, as well as variations in coat color.

ABOVE: WOLVES PLAY ALL THEIR LIVES.

HERE, TWO YEARLING FEMALES PLAY WITH THEIR THREE-YEAR-OLD AUNT

WHILE ANOTHER AUNT LOOKS ON AND A HALF-GROWN PUP GOES ABOUT HER BUSINESS.

THE ELDERLY MALE RESTING NEARBY STILL PLAYS, ALTHOUGH NOT AS

OFTEN OR AS VIGOROUSLY AS HE ONCE DID.

❧

LEFT: DURING PLAY, DOMINANCE RELATIONSHIPS ARE MOMENTARILY PUT ASIDE.

OFFENSIVE AND DEFENSIVE ROLE REVERSALS BETWEEN PLAYMATES ARE FREQUENT — THE

ONE ON THE GROUND SOON BECOMES ONE OF THOSE ON TOP.

61

LEFT: SPECTACULAR LEAPS ARE AN IMPORTANT COMPONENT OF WOLF PLAY. THIS AGILE YOUNG MALE EXECUTES A NEARLY VERTICAL LEAP.

❧

BELOW: GENTLE BITES ARE AN ELEMENT OF NEARLY EVERY PLAY BOUT BETWEEN WOLVES. HERE, AN OLDER MALE INVITES A YOUNGER MALE AND FEMALE TO CHASE HIM, AND THEY MOVE IN TO GRAB HIS TAIL OR HINDQUARTERS.

ABOVE: TAILS WAGGING AND BODIES SQUIRMING, A YOUNG MALE AND FEMALE EXUBERANTLY GREET THE DOMINANT MALE OF THEIR PACK. HE RESPONDS WITH TAIL WAGS OF HIS OWN. SUCH DISPLAYS OF AFFECTION ARE MORE COMMON IN WOLF SOCIAL BEHAVIOR THAN AGGRESSION.

❧

RIGHT: WOLVES ENGAGE IN VIGOROUS ROUGH AND TUMBLE PLAY WITH MANY SPILLS.

AN OLDER PUP BEGGING FOR FOOD INTERRUPTS THREE PLAYING ADULTS.

SOME MIGHT SEE THIS PHOTOGRAPH IN TERMS OF DOMINANCE ASSERTION,
INTERPRETING IT TO MEAN THAT EITHER A SUBDOMINANT WOLF IS EXPOSING ITS THROAT
TO A MORE DOMINANT ONE, OR THAT A DOMINANT WOLF IS DARING A SUBDOMINANT TO BITE
HIM IN THE THROAT. IN TRUTH, THESE TWO ADULT MALES ARE ENGAGED IN A FRIENDLY GAME OF
SCRUFF BITE, WHERE THE ROLES OF WHO BITES WHOM ARE FREQUENTLY REVERSED.

WOLVES' FACIAL EXPRESSIONS CONVEY THEIR MOODS.

TWO MALES GREET EACH OTHER WITH EARS BACK, AND RELAXED,

OPEN-MOUTHED, FRIENDLY FACES.

RIGHT: SUBTLE FACIAL EXPRESSIONS REVEAL THE DOMINANCE STATUS OF TWO MALES IN A FACE-TO-FACE ENCOUNTER. THE WOLF ON THE LEFT EXHIBITS THE "PUSHED FORWARD" LOOK OF A DOMINANT BY TURNING HIS EARS TO THE FRONT, PURSING HIS LIPS, AND STARING DIRECTLY AT THE OTHER MALE. THE WOLF ON THE RIGHT REACTS WITH THE "PULLED BACK" EXPRESSION OF A SUBDOMINANT BY PUTTING HIS EARS SLIGHTLY DOWN AND BACK, PULLING THE CORNERS OF HIS MOUTH BACK INTO A CLOSED MOUTH GRIMACE, AND AVERTING HIS GAZE.

LEFT: SCRUFF BITE IS A FAVORITE GAME OF WOLVES. ONE WILL MANEUVER TO GRAB HOLD OF THE OTHER'S SCRUFF, WHILE HIS PLAY PARTNER TRIES INVENTIVE TECHNIQUES TO BREAK THE HOLD.

ALTHOUGH WOLVES ARE SOCIAL BY NATURE, THEY SOMETIMES VENTURE

OFF FOR A SOLITARY EXCURSION THROUGH THE WOODS.

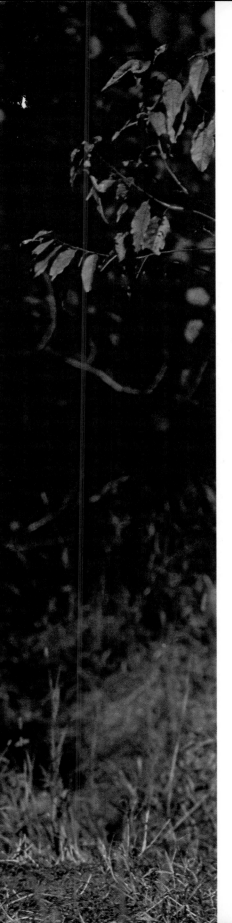

PREDATOR
AND PREY

T HERE'S DETERMINATION IN THEIR GAIT AS THE WOLVES LOPE across the Arctic tundra. The brief northern summer has melted the snow and their thick white coats stand out against the drab greens and grays of the end-less barrens. Nearly four hours from the den they gather on a knoll and look down upon the quarry that enticed them so far from home—three burly musk-oxen grazing on the treeless terrain.

The alpha pair leads the ambush. Frantically, the startled musk-oxen bunch together and turn to face their attackers. The wolves encircle the prey, jumping in, jumping out, as the heavy-horned musk-oxen lunge and retreat. Suddenly, one panics and breaks from the group, the alpha male nipping at its hindquar-ters. Again the musk-oxen join forces and stand their ground—700 pounds (318 kg) of shag, horns, and hooves looming over their small antagonists,

LEFT: THE NOISY FLIGHT OF RAVENS OVERHEAD CAPTURES THE ATTENTION OF THIS MALE.

RAVENS BENEFIT FROM THEIR ASSOCIATION WITH WOLVES, OFTEN SCAVENGING ON THEIR KILLS.

RAVEN CALLS SOMETIMES ALERT WOLVES TO INJURED OR DEAD ANIMALS.

clouds of hot breath huffing through flared nostrils. One wolf charges, but the nervous trio refuses to budge.

Weary and frustrated, the hunters flop down to summon fresh strength. The musk-oxen anxiously pace the tundra in anticipation of another assault. After forty-five minutes all seven wolves get up and leave. These big bulls were never their first choice: it's the calves they want.

Five miles (8 km) across the open land a much larger herd—with at least three calves—is grazing in the midday sun. Silently, the wolves stalk them, gaining ground before they're noticed. The alpha pair leads the onslaught, frightening the herd into a full gallop. One hapless calf is singled out and yanked from its protectors; its mother, confused and terrified, opts for the safety of the herd and keeps running, abandoning her ill-fated offspring.

One wolf grabs it by the hind leg while the others chase the herd, trying to separate a second calf. They give up and return to help bring down the first calf. With multiple sets of vicelike jaws clenched around its face, head, and shoulders, the young musk-ox struggles in vain for five agonizing minutes.

The alphas immediately claim the carcass, warding off their packmates with bites and snarls as they settle down to gorge themselves. The snow-white fur on their faces, chests, and forepaws is stained blood-red. Meekly, the subordinates crawl to the dominant pair, whimpering, pawing, begging for a share of the meat. Eventually everyone finds a place at the carcass.

Tired and satiated, the wolves rest before tearing off scraps of flesh and burying them for a time when food is less bountiful. Stomachs bulging, they begin the 30-mile (48 km) trek back to the den, where the pups and their babysitter await a regurgitated taste of musk-ox.

Since the birth of the pups in May, these wolves have been tied to the den. Snowshoe hares have sustained the family for nearly four months. As the last days of summer fade into fall, this bleak and barren landscape will soon be covered with snow. The wolves face an unforgiving season of feast and famine—dinner may be a weekly event. The pups now are strong enough to travel and soon will help with the hunt: it is time to take larger prey.

Whether wolves live in the frigid north or milder south, catching fresh meat is their main occupation. Unlike omnivorous bears that devour anything from berries and roots to elk and salmon, wolves are true carnivores. Their simple stomachs are unable to digest the thick cellulose of most plants. Though they occasionally eat fruit, grasses, herbs, and mushrooms, they subsist almost entirely on the protein and fat of meat.

A ravenous wolf might consume 10 or 15 pounds (5 or 7 kg) of meat in one sitting, then lie down for a three- or four-hour snooze. These gluttonous bouts inevitably occur after hours of hunting and days of fasting; the wolves are exhausted and famished. Some have been known to sleep eighteen hours after a hunt and hard-earned meal.

The wolf has evolved physically and psychologically to hunt. While it can manage on beavers, racoons, hares, or birds, its whole nature is geared toward stalking, chasing, and killing ungulates, the largest animals in the woods. With so many mouths to feed, and such prolonged periods of privation, the wolf couldn't possibly survive solely on rabbits and rodents.

One of the world's most proficient predators, the wolf is superbly designed to catch animals on the move. With legs longer than most canines, it easily breaks through deep snow. Large feet with calloused toe and heel pads grip rocks, fallen trees, and other rough surfaces when running. It can jump a stream 15 feet (4.6 m) wide and run 40 miles (64 km) an hour for twenty or thirty minutes. One radio-tagged wolf chased a deer at high speed for 13 miles (21 km).

Once a wolf overtakes its quarry, it sinks its teeth into a hind leg or rump to bring it down. Each jaw is equipped with twenty-one teeth—front fangs to hold prey, incisors to tear open a carcass and rip off chunks of flesh, carnassials to slice and chew.

Despite its forbidding weaponry, the wolf is successful in its attacks about one in ten times. Predator and prey have evolved together: as the wolf's efficiency improves through the millennia, so too do the ungulate's escape skills. Many of the wolf's prey species are more fleet-footed than their pursuer, but the wolf has the advantage of endurance. Though it may lose sight of its faster quarry from time to time, a stalwart wolf can run a deer or caribou for hours. As long as the competition stays even, both will endure.

The wolf betters its chances by targeting specific animals. Calves are small and defenseless; old, arthritic adults are slow; others are weakened by diseases, injuries, parasites, or malnutrition. By culling inferior animals the wolf strengthens the herd, unknowingly improving its own prospects for long-term survival. Rarely does a wolf take an animal in its prime, and then only when conditions are ideal. An exception may be healthy male ungulates that become worn down by intense rutting competition.

Size and composition of the herd, terrain, and severity of the wolves' hunger are factors that determine hunting strategies. When an animal is chosen, the wolves sneak up, attempting to gain ground undetected. If the quarry notices them and bolts, the wolves take off in pursuit of it; if it hesitates, the wolves hold back. Panic-stricken animals on the run are the safest bet; those that stand firm could be dangerous.

The pack may lie down around a standing ungulate, testing its aggression. The leaders dart in as if to attack, then retreat if the animal charges or refuses to move. If repeated attempts are resisted, the wolves' energy is better expended on easier prey. Finding the right one, however, could require the testing of several animals. Though the success of a hunt can be decided with one animal failing a momentary test, hours might be spent finding that animal.

Whether wolves plan their attacks or simply respond to the circumstances is unknown. They do seem to relish the stimulation of a fleeing animal, and they undoubtedly show some prudence in choosing their prey. Sometimes an animal is taken by surprise when one wolf is set up as a decoy, distracting the animal while the other wolves move in from behind.

Almost without exception large prey are taken from the rear, the safest place to grab without getting battered by hooves or gored by antlers. When the animal stops running, it is usually brought down by the head, generally the nose, while other wolves tear at the flanks, neck, and throat. Some animals succumb quickly; others linger in obstinate anguish.

Each species has its own idiosyncrasies and presents different hazards and challenges to a hungry wolf. A moose, the largest prey, can break the back of a wolf that unwisely gets behind its ponderous rear hooves. At 1,800 pounds (816 kg), a bull moose is the world's largest stag. It counts on its size and strength to repulse predators. Like a horse, it can keep up a good pace for a long time, outrunning a comparatively slow wolf.

Elk and caribou, though smaller than moose, can also deliver a nasty wallop with their hooves or puncture a wolf's skin with pointed antlers. Both species form large herds, relying on safety in numbers. Caribou try to avoid wolves in calving season by dispersing to secluded islands or ridges. Calves are particularly vulnerable on the day of birth when they're unable to run. Within days, cows with calves give up their isolation and join nursery herds where sheer numbers deter wolves from attacking.

Unlike elk or moose, deer fight with pointed front hooves, rearing up on hind legs and stabbing forward, occasionally piercing a wolf's chest or skull. Some deer gather in winter "yards" where the safety-in-numbers tactic prevails. During other times of the year, herds disband and individuals become harder to find. When foraging alone, their best defense is speed.

Mountain sheep depend on butting power when confronted. Like mountain goats, however, their enviable agility in steep and rugged terrain usually protects them from wolves.

Bison, the historic mainstay of North American wolves, employ similar defense strategies as musk-oxen. Rumps together, oversized heads lowered, they point their short, curved horns toward the aggressors while holding fast in a circle. Calves are neatly stashed in the center, protected by the adults' mammothlike bodies.

Thanks to human help, wolves once again hunt bison in the northern Canadian wilderness. In the early 1800s North American bison numbered 50 or 60 million. Wholesale slaughter by European settlers reduced them to near extinction by 1885, taking wolf numbers down with them. They were protected under Canadian law in 1894. In 1922, Wood Buffalo National Park, on the Alberta-Northwest Territories border, was set aside as a refuge for the continent's last herd of wood bison, about fifteen hundred animals.

Supplemented by transplants from other remnant herds, bison in the park numbered some five thousand in the early 1980s when Dr. Lu Carbyn, of the Canadian Wildlife Service, documented wolf attacks on bison calves. In a paper co-authored by T. Trottier, Carbyn describes an eleven-hour ordeal in which four wolves repeatedly attacked a calf, only to be driven back each time by its mother and young bulls. The story is a poignant portrayal of the tenacity of both predator and prey when faced with a life-or-death crisis.

It was an early morning in May. The wolves had been testing several small herds for three days before launching their first unsuccessful assault. An hour later they brought down the calf, but it managed to break free and rejoin the herd. In the first three hours the calf was attacked eight times.

> The calf, with the cow at its side, was repeatedly rushed by the wolves. Two wolves downed the calf (sixth time), but it squirmed out and took off running. Three wolves pulled the calf down again (seventh time), but again the adult bison chased them off. . . . The alpha wolf persisted, finally grabbing the calf again (eighth time), before being chased off by the cow. The downed calf rose slowly this time and stood weakly. The calf appeared to be wounded in several places.
>
> Chases back and forth continued. The calf walked stiffly, limping; yet it could still run and seemed to have the stamina to resort to short bursts of speed when needed. . . . Examination of the calf through binoculars revealed wounds on the upper left front leg

near the chest. The forehead was bloody, and conspicuous wounds were present on the lower hind legs. The upper right hind leg was noticeably swollen.

After a futile eleventh attempt, the haggard wolves abandoned the chase. The beleaguered calf appeared to recover over the next two days, but it is not known if gangrene set into its wounds.

The attacks occurred in late spring when the persistent wolves probably had pups to feed. Proximity of prey is an important consideration in selecting den sites. A survey of 209 dens in the Northwest Territories found that 60 percent were within 31 miles (50 km) of the northern treeline, where caribou forage through the pupping season. Ninety-three percent of seven hundred wolf scats collected near twelve dens contained caribou hair. It's interesting to note that muscle tissue from wolves and caribou here contained traces of radioactive cesium, thought to have entered the environment through nuclear bomb tests in the 1950s, and from the 1986 Chernobyl nuclear accident. One of the most active and electropositive metals, cesium collects in lichens eaten by ungulates and concentrates as it moves up the food chain.

Long-term effects of wolf predation on big game are the subject of numerous studies, some which suggest that the so-called "balance of nature" can be thrown seriously out of whack. In the late 1970s, British Columbia biologists were perplexed by declines of caribou in the Spatsizi wilderness, in the northern part of the province. Calves born in June seemed to disappear within a month. Wolf scats were found to consist entirely of caribou, even though moose were available. It was discovered that wolves, wolverines, and grizzlies were severely depleting the caribou.

When prey is abundant wolves are known to practise "surplus killing," bringing down ungulates and then eating only the choicest organs—tongue, liver, or heart. A pregnant doe is occasionally sacrificed for the fetus. Although the carcasses feed ravens, weasels, coyotes, and other scavengers, it is not the efficient predation depicted in biology textbooks.

Cyril Shelford, former trapper, hunting guide, rancher, and British Columbia agriculture minister, is a resolute advocate of wolf control. As early as the 1930s he began to document surplus killing at his ranch and guiding territory in central British Columbia. In 1939 he followed fifteen deer running from a pack of five wolves; within 4 miles (6 km) fourteen deer were dead and uneaten. Another year he found seventy-nine untouched deer carcasses. One weekend he discovered fifty-four dead caribou that had been chased into heavy snow and killed. By the mid-1980s, Shelford estimated that wolves had reduced the game populations in his region by 90 percent in the previous ten or fifteen years.

North America's longest predator-prey study began at Michigan's Isle Royale National Park in 1957. Moose had been enjoying a predator-free existence until the late 1940s or early '50s when mainland wolves apparently walked across frozen Lake Superior to take up residence on the 210-square-mile (544 km²) island.

Numbers of both species increased. By 1970 there were an estimated eighteen wolves and twelve hundred moose. The moose population crashed the next year, falling to fewer than eight hundred. Wolves continued to climb but suddenly dropped in 1977 from forty-two to thirty-three. They recovered, increasing to fifty by 1980 when moose numbered about six hundred. Then the moose situation improved while wolves declined. By 1992, the moose population was estimated at sixteen hundred, the highest since the study began. Meanwhile, wolves dropped to a mere dozen. These wide swings in numbers suggest the "balance of nature" is a complex phenomenon: it is not a matter of predators simply rising and falling in harmony with their prey.

OPPOSITE PAGE: GROUP LIVING PROVIDES ADVANTAGES FOR BOTH PREDATOR AND PREY.

WHEREAS THE PACK IS IMPORTANT TO THE WOLF'S HUNTING SUCCESS,

THE HERD, IN TURN, PROVIDES DEFENSE FOR THESE ELK.

❧

INSET: THE ABILITY TO DETECT MOTION IS THE MOST

IMPORTANT ASPECT OF THE WOLF'S SENSE OF VISION.

HEALTHY PREY ANIMALS CAN EASILY ELUDE WOLVES IN MOST CIRCUMSTANCES.

THOSE THAT ARE SICK OR INJURED MOVE DIFFERENTLY AND PROVIDE WOLVES WITH

VISUAL CLUES AS TO WHICH INDIVIDUALS MIGHT BE SUCCESSFULLY HUNTED.

LEFT: THE CLEAR, SMOOTH SURFACE OF A ROCKY
MOUNTAIN POND PROVIDES A MIRROR IMAGE OF THIS MALE
HUNTING THE SHORELINE IN SPRING.

❧

BELOW: WOLVES HUNT BOTH AQUATIC AND LAND ANIMALS
ALONG THE BANKS OF RIVERS AND STREAMS. ALTHOUGH
WOLVES CAN SWIM AFTER PREY, THEIR PROFICIENCY AT
HUNTING LIES ON THE LAND, NOT IN THE WATER. THIS
ADULT MALE HUNTING IN THE ROCKY MOUNTAINS MAKES
AN UNSUCCESSFUL LUNGE AT A BEAVER.

ABOVE: WOLVES OFTEN HUNT ALONE FOR SMALL ANIMALS,

ESPECIALLY IN SPRING AND SUMMER WHEN RODENTS ARE PLENTIFUL.

❧

RIGHT: ALTHOUGH WOLVES NEED LARGE UNGULATES IN THEIR DIET TO SURVIVE,

THEY ALSO EAT SMALLER PREY SUCH AS WOODCHUCKS AND OTHER RODENTS.

85

UNLIKE HUMANS, WOLVES CANNOT SWEAT THROUGH THEIR SKIN AND

MUST DISSIPATE EXCESSIVE BODY HEAT IN OTHER WAYS, MOSTLY THROUGH PANTING.

ABOVE: PUPS CONTINUE TO BEG FOR FOOD EVEN WHEN
THEY ARE OLD ENOUGH TO ACCOMPANY ADULTS ON HUNTING FORAYS.

RIGHT: WOLVES DRINK BY CUPPING THEIR TONGUES OUTWARD AND LAPPING
WATER INTO THEIR MOUTHS. IN WINTER, WOLVES MAKE HOLES IN THE ICE TO
REACH THE WATER BELOW, OR EAT SNOW WHEN THE ICE IS TOO THICK.

ABOVE: WOLVES HAVE SETS OF LONG TACTILE VIBRISSAE, OR WHISKERS, ON THEIR CHINS,
THE SIDES OF THEIR MUZZLES, AND ABOVE THEIR EYES. THESE SURROUND THE FACE
AND SERVE AS SENSITIVE FEELERS IN TIGHT, DARK PLACES.

❧

RIGHT: THIS MIXED DECIDUOUS AND EVERGREEN FOREST NEAR THE GREAT LAKES IS TYPICAL
WOLF COUNTRY. WOLVES DEPEND ON WELL-KNOWN TRAILS, MENTAL MAPS, LANDMARKS,
AND SCENT MARKS TO NAVIGATE THROUGH THEIR TERRITORIES.

A STALKING WOLF LOWERS HIS HEAD AND MOVES QUIETLY AND SMOOTHLY,

MAKING AS LITTLE VERTICAL MOVEMENT AS POSSIBLE SO AS NOT TO ALERT HIS QUARRY.

WOLVES TRAVEL LONG DISTANCES IN A FLUID, EFFORTLESS GAIT

AND CAN ATTAIN SPEEDS OF 40 MILES PER HOUR (65 KPH).

LEFT: BIGHORN SHEEP FORAGE ON WINDSWEPT, SNOW-FREE SLOPES WHERE THEY ARE VULNERABLE TO WOLF ATTACK. HOWEVER, THEY CAN ESCAPE TO THE STEEP, ROCKY TERRAIN ABOVE WHERE THE LESS SURE-FOOTED WOLVES HAVE DIFFICULTY FOLLOWING.

BELOW: HOOVED ANIMALS, SUCH AS WHITE-TAILED DEER, MOOSE, AND ELK, MAKE UP MOST OF THE WOLF'S DIET.

ABOVE: THESE PACK MEMBERS HAVE CARRIED PIECES OF DEER AWAY FROM THE CARCASS, WHERE FEEDING CLOSE TOGETHER CAN LEAD TO AGGRESSION. DOMINANT WOLVES ARE MORE LIKELY TO STAY AT THE CARCASS AND FEED ON THE PREFERRED PARTS UNTIL THEY ARE SATIATED. THE SUBDOMINANTS THEN MOVE IN TO TAKE THEIR TURN.

છ

RIGHT: THESE TWO WOLVES THREATEN EACH OTHER AT A CARCASS BY NARROWING THEIR EYES AND PULLING THEIR NOSEPADS UP AND BACK SHARPLY, EXPOSING THE TEETH.

A SCENT TRAIL HAS LED THIS MALE TO A TREE.

RIGHT: AN EIGHT-MONTH-OLD PUP IN ITS FIRST WINTER FOCUSES ON
A RODENT TUNNELING BENEATH THE SNOW. WOLVES CAN HEAR THE ULTRASONIC
VOCALIZATIONS PRODUCED BY RODENTS EVEN THOUGH THEY CANNOT
VOCALIZE IN THE ULTRASONIC RANGE THEMSELVES.

❧

BELOW: WOLVES ARE REMARKABLY TOLERANT OF RAVENS.
RAVENS HAVE BEEN OBSERVED HOPPING AROUND RESTING WOLVES, PECKING
THEM AND PULLING THEIR TAILS, UNTIL THE WOLVES BECAME
ANNOYED AND LUNGED AT THEM.

SNOWSHOE HARES ARE SO PLENTIFUL AND REPRODUCE SO RAPIDLY THAT THEY

ARE A STABLE FOOD SOURCE FOR MANY CARNIVORES IN NORTHERN AREAS, INCLUDING WOLVES.

CATCHING THEM IS NOT EASY, THOUGH, AS THE FASTER AND MORE AGILE HARES

ARE ABLE TO ELUDE THEIR LARGER PURSUERS WITH EASE IN MOST CHASES.

THE SLENDER LEGS AND LIGHT BODIES OF WOLVES ARE DESIGNED FOR SPEED AND ENDURANCE.

MASSIVE LEGS AND BODIES, LIKE THOSE OF LARGE CATS, WOULD ONLY SLOW WOLVES DOWN

OVER THE LONG DISTANCES THEY PURSUE THEIR PREY.

ABOVE: GRIZZLY BEARS AND WOLVES SHARE THE SAME REMOTE WILDERNESS AREAS.

BOTH NEED LARGE EXPANSES OF WILD COUNTRY FOR SURVIVAL.

❧

OPPOSITE PAGE: BEARS LEAVE SCENT STATIONS FOR EACH OTHER

BY SCRATCHING AND RUBBING ON TREES. THIS YEARLING WOLF INVESTIGATES

A RECENT RUB BY A BEAR THAT PASSED BY BEFORE HIM.

ABOVE: COUGARS AND WOLVES SHARE HABITATS AND

PREY SPECIES BUT LIVE AND HUNT IN VERY DIFFERENT WAYS.

THE MASSIVELY BUILT COUGAR BRINGS DOWN ITS PREY QUICKLY AND ALONE.

THE LIGHTER WOLF WORKS WITH OTHER PACK MEMBERS TO BRING DOWN LARGE PREY.

❧

LEFT: A WOLF WRAPS HIMSELF AROUND A TREE WHILE

SCENT RUBBING AN INTERESTING ODOR.

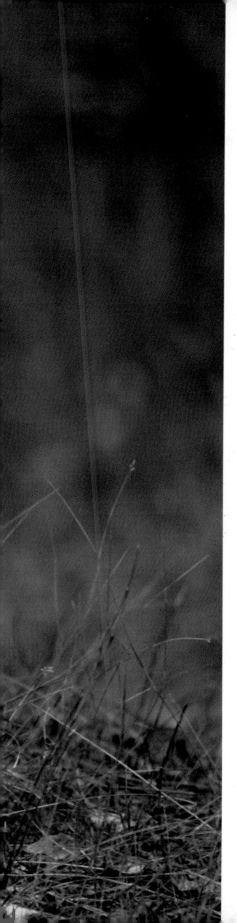

SAVING

THE WOLF

IN 1973 THE WOLF SPECIALIST GROUP OF THE INTERNATIONAL Union for Conservation of Nature and Natural Resources (IUCN) drafted a Wolf Manifesto which stated: "Wolves, like all other wildlife, have a right to exist in a wild state. This right is in no way related to their known value to mankind. Instead, it derives from the right of all living creatures to co-exist with man as part of natural ecosystems."

Seventeen years later, the IUCN published an "Action Plan" that calls for the reintroduction of wolves to their old domains. Such an idea was considered ludicrous only a few decades ago. But by 1990, when the plan was drafted, public understanding of wild creatures and their environmental needs had become more sophisticated. Now, with the intrinsic value of wild animals universally acknowledged, the tradition of managing wildlife only as a harvestable resource is changing. Philosophies like that of the IUCN are embraced in new

LEFT: WOLVES CAN CONVEY THEIR EMOTIONAL STATE BY VARIATIONS

IN THE PITCH AND MODULATION OF THEIR HOWLS.

wildlife-management policies. Wildlife viewing, habitat enhancement, and preservation have become higher priorities. Yet even today, while the distinguished scientists of the IUCN lobby to save the wolf, North American governments are still killing wolves to beef up big-game herds.

The scientific community is divided over the controversial use of predator control to enhance game populations for hunters. Right or wrong, the argument at least has some biological basis. In early times only fear, loathing, and ignorance led to the relentless slaughter of the world's wolves.

If Carolus Linnaeus had waited much beyond 1758 to name the wolf *Canis lupus*, he would have found few wolves left to name, at least in his neck of the woods. Linnaeus was the Swedish botanist who created the scientific system of naming plants and animals. When he died in 1778, wolves were extinct in much of Europe and all of Great Britain.

European and British settlers in the New World brought their hatred of wolves with them. The wolf was persecuted throughout its entire range from Mexico to the Arctic. In 1630, Americans in Massachusetts paid their first bounty. A hundred and sixty-three years later, in 1793, the parliament of Upper Canada passed An Act to Encourage the Destruction of Wolves and Bears.

The shoot-on-sight attitude prevailed for over three more centuries and was espoused even by some of the continent's most respected proponents of wildlife preservation. William Hornaday, of the New York Zoological Society, described the wolf as "strong of limb and jaw, insatiable in appetite, a master of cunning and the acme of cruelty . . . wherever found, the proper course with the wolf is to kill it as quickly as possible."

Hornaday's sentiments were shared by J. Dewey Soper, an eminent Canadian naturalist who died in 1982. "If we want dead wolves, does it much matter within reason how they become defunct?" he wrote. "The answer is comparably simple—kill them."

From the 1870s a rigorous fifty-year campaign to annihilate the wolf swept through the North American wilderness. Private and government-sponsored bounties were paid on thousands of wolves. One by one they were poisoned, trapped, and hunted. Farmers and ranchers usurped their habitat and hunters shot their prey.

When the carnage began in earnest, wolves had already been wiped out in New Brunswick and Nova Scotia. On the Prairies they disappeared with the buffalo before the turn of the century. Not a wolf was left on the island of Newfoundland by 1911. Farming helped squeeze them from southern Quebec and Ontario. Bounties, ranching, and urbanization extirpated wolves from much of British Columbia.

The situation was similar in the contiguous United States where wolves virtually vanished from the South and East, and became a rarity in the West and northern Midwest. Official government exterminators were triumphant in their crusade against wolves in Yellowstone National Park, the first great American wilderness to be preserved for generations of the future.

By the start of the 1930s the exterminators were victorious. Like cougars, eagles, and other verminous predators, wolves were too few to cause much trouble. But the respite was short-lived: between the 1930s and '50s wolves began to repopulate old haunts, particularly from the Great Lakes to Alaska.

The wolf-eliminators dusted off their traps, reloaded their shotguns, and freshened the bait at poison stations. "Needless to say, the control of predators is not only a perplexing problem but a contentious one as well, and we are satisfied from the investigations that we have made that the problem of predators will not be settled through the payment of bounties alone," says the 1949 report of the British Columbia Predator Control Division. "The employment of scientific personnel and trained predatory-animal hunters is a must if the demands of the public in general are to be coped with and the welfare of our game populations is to be protected."

Governments across the continent agreed. Losses of big game and livestock to wolves would not be tolerated. The obliteration of wolves was especially sedulous in the southern states and Mexico, where they were eradicated from 95 percent of their original range. By the time Minnesota dropped its bounty in 1965, it was one of the few states with wolves as part of the natural fauna.

While predator-control programs continued through the 1970s and '80s, a groundswell of resistance was building. It was an era of environmental awareness; the public loudly voiced its repugnance at poisoning wolves with strychnine and Compound 1080, shooting them from the air, and snaring them in leg-hold traps.

International outrage erupted in 1984 when it was discovered that the British Columbia government was shooting wolves from helicopters to boost big-game herds for hunters. Conservationists from across Canada, the United States, Britain, and Europe rallied to the rescue of the wolf. Canadian embassies, airline terminals, and ferry docks were picketed; tourist outlets were blacklisted; oil companies that fuelled the helicopters were boycotted; and snow-shoed protesters travelled through the northern outback to hamper government wolf-killers. Of the 8,764 people who signed letters and petitions, only 121 sided with the government.

Unwilling to become embroiled in similar controversies, wildlife managers in other jurisdictions became more sensitive to public concerns about predator control. Wolves would still be killed to protect livestock and game, but not without public scrutiny. British Columbia eventually set up a Wolf Working Group, which includes members from the public and conservation groups, to recommend when wolf control is needed. Plans in the early 1990s to eradicate wolves in big-game areas of Alaska and the Yukon have met with intense opposition.

The long-term effectiveness of control programs is questionable: if habitat and prey exist, repressed wolf populations invariably bounce back. Numbers in the United States, excluding Alaska, are still low, but they are nonetheless increasing. In the early 1990s there are an estimated sixteen hundred wolves in Minnesota, the only state among the lower forty-eight where they are not officially endangered. Immigration to neighboring Wisconsin and Michigan has brought wolf numbers there up to about sixty in total. In Montana and other northwestern states, there may be fewer than fifty, but wolves from Canada appear to be dispersing into those states. The 1988 introduction of eight red wolves to North Carolina seems to be successful. If there are any wolves in Mexico, they likely number fewer than a dozen.

The species has fared better above the forty-ninth parallel. Alaska today has a healthy population of seven thousand or more. In Canada, where wolves occupy about 85 percent of their traditional range, the total population is estimated at fifty thousand to sixty-five thousand. Numbers are greatest in the Northwest Territories—perhaps as high as fifteen thousand—where they roam across all of their former range. There are about eight thousand wolves in British Columbia, five thousand in the Yukon, and at least four thousand in Alberta. Saskatchewan has more than four thousand, and Manitoba has about six thousand. There are well over ten thousand in Ontario and Quebec. In Labrador, where they exist in 95 percent of their original range, the population could be as high as five thousand.

Alaska and Canada show the most promise for the preservation of wolves, and dispersal into the northern United States is improving populations there. In spite of these encouraging numbers, conservationists are not complacent about the future of North American wolves. In *Wild Hunters: Predators in Peril*, Sherry Pettigrew and Monte Hummel, of World Wildlife Fund Canada, warn that predator control continues to jeopardize the future of wolves. If the species is to remain an integral part of North American ecosystems, "the only safe conservation route is to stop large-scale wolf-killing programs altogether."

> Simply put, the biggest threat to wolves is people who are not prepared to share food and wilderness territory with them. We establish our farms in wolf habitat, then, when the wolf does what comes naturally by eating our livestock, our answer is to get rid of the wolf. Since the wolf hunts the same animals as human hunters, again our answer is to get rid of the wolf. In effect, by killing the wolf we're trying to get rid of the competition. And as long as wolves are seen as competitors, as long as we are unprepared to share with them, there will be pressure to reduce wolf numbers. Whether they take the form of wolf-control programs or habitat disturbance, these activities against the wolf are all secondary spinoffs of basic human intolerance.

Pettigrew and Hummel contend that wolf-control decisions are based on several unproven notions—that specific ungulate populations are limited by wolves; that predictable increases in ungulates will result from reducing wolves; that prey will sink to "undesirable" levels if wolves are not controlled. They question the predictability of control programs and ask if wolves are being killed when ungulates suffer from harsh weather, food shortages, and other factors that cannot be controlled. And in Canada, where only one in ten people hunt, how desirable is it to artificially raise ungulate numbers for hunters?

They agree, however, that northern wolf populations can sustain hunting and trapping if seasons, bag limits, and regional regulations are strictly observed. Seasons and bag limits for prey species should also vary to coincide with fluctuations in ungulate populations. Rather than kill wolves when ungulate numbers are down, there should be lean years and good years for hunters, just as there are for predators.

If predator control is to be permitted where wolves take livestock, farmers and ranchers must first attempt to protect their animals. Fences and proper disposal of carcasses should discourage wolf predation. There are also several breeds of guard dogs available to protect livestock.

World Wildlife Fund estimates that only 1.2 percent of Canada's wolf range lies within parks and other protected areas and that less than 3 percent of the country's wolves inhabit those areas. Many that stray beyond park boundaries are taken by hunters and trappers. About 30 percent of the wolves in Ontario's Algonquin Park, for example, are killed each year when they follow deer outside the park to winter yards. Among World Wildlife Fund's boldest recommendations is the establishment of protected areas adjoining parks and wilderness reserves where hunting, trapping, and predator control would be prohibited.

American conservationists support the concept and suggest that travel corridors for wolves dispersing to new areas be preserved. For example, wolves moving from Minnesota to form new packs in Wisconsin appear to favor one particular route. By regulating the development of highways, fences, housing, and other impediments, the free movement of wolves can be assured.

Under existing wildlife management, even parks cannot guarantee the unimpaired mobility of animals. Heavy tourism around downtown Banff, in Alberta's Banff National Park, now threatens to block wildlife travel through the park's main valley.

Several state and provincial governments are leaning toward a zone system as a means for wolves and humans to coexist. Under such a scheme there would be areas where no wolves could be killed and others where killing would be allowed for specific reasons. Wolves and prey would be given complete protection in parks and reserves; hunting and trapping would be permitted outside the reserves. When regulated by seasons and bag limits, hunting and trapping could be methods of controlling errant wolves. Wolf control would be practised in livestock areas and farmers would be compensated for losses. In Minnesota, where wolves share a 25,000-square-mile (64 000 km²) range with domestic cattle and sheep, a zone system has been in place for several years.

The consensus among wolf researchers is that natural immigration from one area to another is the best chance for the return of the North American wolf to its traditional range. In some areas, however, reintroductions are warranted and the U.S. government has appointed special wolf-recovery teams to help bring wolves back to the wild.

The red wolf, the most endangered canid in the world, was almost extinct in 1977 when fourteen were taken to the Point Defiance Zoo in Tacoma,

Washington, to start a breeding population. A decade later some eighty captive red wolves were held at eight U.S. locations. The first reintroduction was at North Carolina's Alligator River National Wildlife Refuge, where eight wolves were released in 1988. At least eight or ten other sites are needed to give the red wolf a new chance in its old habitat.

A recovery plan for the Mexican wolf, declared endangered in 1976, has been approved, but opposition from state governments has prevented any releases. Apparently no wild wolves have been born in Arizona since 1944; the last ones were gone from Texas and New Mexico by 1970. Only a handful remained in Mexico in 1977 when a trapper was contracted by the U.S. Fish and Wildlife Service to catch some. Now several are held at the St. Louis Zoo and at the Arizona-Sonora Desert Museum. But pressure from ranchers has kept the wolves incarcerated.

The most ambitious, and perhaps controversial, reintroduction plan is for Yellowstone National Park. Established in 1872, Yellowstone was the birthplace of America's national parks. This 3,470-square-mile (8987 km²) wilderness straddles the borders of Wyoming, Idaho, and Montana, an unscathed mountain outback where the natural flora and fauna are preserved forever. Except the wolf.

"It is evident that the work of controlling these animals must be vigorously prosecuted by the most effective means available whether or not this meets with the approval of certain game conservationists," the park's superintendent stated in 1922. Four years later the last Yellowstone wolf was trapped.

Today, money has been appropriated to study the Yellowstone situation, and legislation has been introduced to bring wolves back. The plan, approved in 1980 and revised in 1987, is to relocate wolves from Canada or Minnesota.

Wolves would be controlled outside the park; the national organization Defenders of Wildlife, has set up a compensation fund for ranchers. Surveys of citizens in Wyoming, where most of the park lies, show almost half in favor of the plan and only 16 percent opposed. But ranchers and others who live near Yellowstone are content with their wolf-free environment and no reintroductions have been done.

History has proven that the future of the wolf is decided by *Homo sapiens*, not *Canis lupus*. As people learn more about the ways of the wolf, the better they are able to direct its fate in North America. Various organizations are devoted to enlightening the public about the habits and needs of the wolf.

The International Wolf Center in Ely, Minnesota provides lectures, exhibits, and audiovisuals. Field trips to find wolf packs and dens, and hear the howl of the wolf are conducted through the center.

Even the most dedicated wolf-seekers rarely see a wolf, but many are satisfied to hear one. Each year naturalists from Ontario's Algonquin Provincial Park take thousands of visitors on howling excursions. Gathered under the moonlight, they listen in silence as a naturalist howls in the hope of eliciting a response. More than half the time there's a reply.

Whoever hears the haunting howl of a wolf is left with an indelible impression. Only in the wildest of places can the call of the wolf be heard. It rings through the woodlands, assuring all who hear that these environs are still intact, that its untamed denizens continue to thrive. With our care, this wild hunter will survive as a symbol of true North American wilderness.

OPPOSITE PAGE: THE DAWN LIGHT HIGHLIGHTS A MALE WOLF IN HIS FALL COAT.

CLEANLINESS IS IMPORTANT TO WOLVES. ONE REASON FOR ENTERING
WATER MAY BE TO WASH DIRT AND OTHER DEBRIS FROM THEIR COATS.

TRAVELLING WOLVES WILL SOMETIMES SWIM OR WADE ACROSS

BODIES OF WATER RATHER THAN TAKE A LONGER LAND ROUTE.

THE COYOTE, ONCE STRICTLY A WESTERN ANIMAL, HAS NOW

ESTABLISHED ITSELF THROUGHOUT NORTH AMERICA FROM COAST TO COAST.

OVER THE PAST CENTURY, COYOTES HAVE SUCCESSFULLY MOVED INTO

AREAS WHERE THERE ARE NO LONGER VIABLE WOLF POPULATIONS.

ALTHOUGH THIS STRIKING TWO-YEAR-OLD MALE'S COAT IS FOR THE MOST PART BLACK,

HE IS STILL CLASSIFIED AS A GRAY, OR TIMBER, WOLF. ONE COLOR MAY PREDOMINATE,

BUT WOLVES' COATS ARE IN FACT A GRADATION OF SEVERAL COLORS.

THESE CAN RANGE FROM NEARLY WHITE TO PREDOMINANTLY CREAM, GRAY, BROWN, OR BLACK.

MANY BLACK WOLVES HAVE WHITE SPOTS ON THEIR CHESTS.

WELL-INSULATED FUR ENABLES WOLVES TO SLEEP COMFORTABLY
OUTSIDE IN FRIGID CONDITIONS. SLEEK GUARD HAIRS COVER THE UNDERCOAT
TO RETAIN WARMTH AND TO REPEL WATER AND SNOW.

EVEN IN COLD WEATHER, STRENUOUS PHYSICAL EXERTION AND THE WARM SUN CAN MAKE WOLVES TOO WARM IN THEIR THICK COATS. THIS WOLF PANTS TO COOL OFF.

SMELL IS THE SENSE WOLVES RELY ON MOST TO INFORM THEM ABOUT THEIR ENVIRONMENT. THE ELONGATED MUZZLE IS A COMPLEX STRUCTURE FOR SAMPLING EVEN MINUTE PARTICLES OF SCENT.

WOLVES' COATS ARE ADAPTED FOR THE CHANGING SEASONS IN NORTHERN CLIMES.

THE THICK, SOFT UNDERCOAT PROVIDES EXCELLENT INSULATION DURING COLD WEATHER

AND IS SHED IN THE SPRING AND SUMMER.

THE CLASSIC FACE OF A GRAY WOLF.

THE CAP OF DARK HAIR ENHANCES THE LIGHT MARKINGS AROUND THE EXPRESSIVE EYES.

THE WHITE CHEEKS WILL BECOME MORE PRONOUNCED AS HIS FUR TURNS LIGHTER WITH AGE.

THE EVENING LIGHT STRIKES THE GOLDEN EYE OF A YOUNG MALE WOLF.

FEW PEOPLE CAN REMAIN UNAFFECTED BY THE BEAUTY INHERENT

IN THE HAUNTING, PENETRATING GAZE OF A WOLF.

WOLVES HAVE SPECIAL FRIENDSHIPS, WHICH ARE CELEBRATED WITH BODY LANGUAGE.

THESE TWO FRIENDS OUT FOR A ROMP LIKE TO MAINTAIN CLOSE CONTACT,

TROTTING SIDE BY SIDE AND BUMPING INTO EACH OTHER.

LEFT: PLANS TO REINTRODUCE WOLVES INTO AREAS OF THEIR HISTORIC RANGE IN THE SOUTHERN ROCKIES ARE ENCOUNTERING STIFF OPPOSITION FROM RANCHERS WORRIED ABOUT LIVESTOCK PREDATION. BECAUSE WOLVES OCCASIONALLY PREY ON LIVESTOCK WHEN THERE IS INSUFFICIENT NATURAL PREY AVAILABLE, RANCHERS' CONCERNS MUST BE TAKEN INTO CONSIDERATION BEFORE WOLVES CAN SAFELY COME BACK TO SOME OF THE PLACES THEY ONCE LIVED. RESEARCHERS ARE WORKING ON NON-LETHAL DETERRENTS TO LIVESTOCK PREDATION TO HELP BOTH THE RANCHERS AND THE WOLVES.

❧

BELOW: WOLVES CAN RECOGNIZE THE HOWLS OF OTHER WOLVES THEY KNOW JUST AS HUMANS CAN RECOGNIZE OTHER PEOPLE'S VOICES.

125

SELECTED BIBLIOGRAPHY

Bass, Rick. *The Ninemile Wolves*. New York: Ballantine, 1992.

Carbyn, Ludwig N. *Gray Wolf* and *Red Wolf*. Edmonton: Canadian Wildlife Service,1987.

____. "A Delicate Balancing Act." Toronto: *Outdoor Canada*, June/July 1985.

Carbyn, Ludwig N., and Trottier, T. *Descriptions of Wolf Attacks on Bison Calves in Wood Buffalo National Park*. Calgary: Arctic Institute of North America, 1988.

Coscia, Elizabeth M. et al. "Spectral Analysis of Neonatal Wolf *Canis Lupus* Vocalizations." *The International Journal of Animal Sound and Its Recording*, Vol. 3, 1991.

Fentress, John C. et al. *A Multidimensional Approach to Agonistic Behavior in Wolves*. Dordrecht, Netherlands: Dr. W. Junk Publishers, 1987.

Ginsberg, J. R. and Macdonald, D. W. *Foxes, Wolves, Jackals, and Dogs*. Gland, Switzerland: IUCN, 1990.

Harrington, Fred H. *Monogamy in Wolves*. Park Ridge, NJ: Noyes Publications, 1982.

Hellier, Robin, and Brandenburg, Jim. *White Wolf* (film). Washington, DC: National Geographic Society, 1988.

Hummel, Monte, and Pettigrew, Sherry. *Wild Hunters: Predators in Peril*. Toronto: Key Porter Books, 1991.

International Wolf Center. "The 1993 Plans for Alaska Wolf Management." *International Wolf*, Vol. 3, No. 4, Winter 1993.

Keiter, Robert B., and Boyce, Mark S. *The Greater Yellowstone Ecosystem: Redefining America's Wilderness Heritage*. New Haven: Yale University Press, 1991.

Lawrence, R. D. *Trail of the Wolf*. Toronto: Key Porter Books, 1993.

Lopez, Barry H. *Of Wolves and Men*. New York: Charles Scribner's Sons, 1978.

MacNeill, Paul. "Call of the Wolves." *The Novascotian*, Oct. 29, 1993.

Mech, L. David. *The Way of the Wolf*. Stillwater, MN: Voyageur Press, 1991.

____. *The Wolf: The Ecology and Behavior of an Endangered Species*. Minneapolis: University of Minnesota Press, 1970.

Murray, John A. *Out Among the Wolves*. Vancouver: Whitecap Books, 1993.

Obee, Bruce. *Coastal Wildlife of British Columbia*. Vancouver: Whitecap Books, 1991.

____. "Wolves of British Columbia: Predator or Prey?" *Wildlife Review*, Vol. X, No. 10, Summer 1984.

Paquet, Paul C., and Fuller, William A. *Scent Marking and Territoriality in Wolves of Riding Mountain National Park*. Toronto: Oxford University Press, 1990.

Ryan, Jenny et al. "Scent rubbing in wolves (*Canis Lupus*): The Effect of Novelty." *Canadian Journal of Zoology*, Vol. 64, 1986.

____ et al. "Wolves' Responses to Conspecific Urine-marks." Edmonton: Second North American Symposium on Wolves, 1992.

Savage, Candace. *Wolves*. Vancouver: Douglas & McIntyre, 1988.

Thiel, Dick. "Preserving Wolf Dispersal and Travel Corridors." *International Wolf*, Vol. 3, No. 1, Spring 1993.

INDEX